5 Minute girls GRATITUDE JOURNAL

100 Day Gratitude Journal for Girls with Daily Journal Prompts, Fun Challenges, and Inspirational Quotes

This Book Belongs to:

_____

5 Minute Girls Gratitude Journal by Gratitude Daily
Published by Creative Ideas Publishing

© 2020 Gratitude Daily

All rights reserved. No portion of this book may be reproduced in any form without permission from the author, except as permitted by U.S. copyright law.

For permissions contact:
permissions@creativeideaspublishing.com

ISBN: 978-1-952016-1-65

HOW TO USE

Hi friend!

Taking a few minutes to fill out this journal each day will help you have a **thankful** and **happy** heart! Keep in mind that you can be thankful for BIG THINGS like family, friends, and exciting events or you can be thankful for small things like a sunny day, a new book, or freshly baked cookies.

If you miss a day, don't worry or be sad! Just do it the next day and **have fun with this new adventure!** XO,

Jori Outlaw

To the right is a journal page that we already filled in as an example.

5 Minute Girls Gratitude Journal

Date __|__|__

One moment that I really enjoyed today was...
_____
_____
_____
_____
_____

Draw something that makes you happy:

Name 3 things you are thankful for today.
1. _____
2. _____
3. _____

TODAY I FEEL
(circle one)

Kindness Challenge
Buy string and beads and make a friendship bracelet for a friend.

5 Minute Girls Gratitude Journal

Date _ _ | _ _ | _ _

One moment that I really enjoyed today was...

Draw something that makes you happy:

1. _____
2. _____
3. _____

name 3 things you are thankful for today.

TODAY I FEEL

(circle one)

Memory-Making Challenge

Go on a nature walk and observe new things.

5 Minute Girls Gratitude Journal

Date __/__/__

One moment that I really enjoyed today was...

Draw something that makes you happy:

1. _____
2. _____
3. _____

Name 3 things you are thankful for today.

TODAY I FEEL

(circle one)

Memory-Making Challenge

Build a fort inside.

5 Minute Girls Gratitude Journal

Date __/__/__

One moment that I really enjoyed today was...

Draw something that makes you happy:

1. _____
2. _____
3. _____

name 3 things you are thankful for today.

TODAY I FEEL

(circle one)

Memory-Making Challenge

Look up at the stars at night and see if anything looks like a smiley face or other image.

5 Minute Girls Gratitude Journal

5 Minute Girls Gratitude Journal

Date __/__/__

One moment that I really enjoyed today was...

Draw something that makes you happy:

1. _____
2. _____
3. _____

name 3 things you are thankful for today.

TODAY I FEEL

(circle one)

Memory-Making Challenge

Ask an adult to help you find a recipe to make your very own playdough.

Date __/__/__

One moment that I really enjoyed today was...

Draw something that makes you happy:

1. _____
2. _____
3. _____

name 3 things you are thankful for today.

TODAY I FEEL
(circle one)

Memory-Making Challenge

Find a tree to climb that you have never climbed before.

5 Minute Girls Gratitude Journal

Date __/__/__

One moment that I really enjoyed today was...

Draw something that makes you happy:

1. _____
2. _____
3. _____

Name 3 things you are thankful for today.

TODAY I FEEL
(circle one)

—— Memory-Making Challenge ——
Play hopscotch.

5 Minute Girls Gratitude Journal

Date __/__/__

One moment that I really enjoyed today was...

Draw something that makes you happy:

1. _____
2. _____
3. _____

name 3 things you are thankful for today.

TODAY I FEEL

(circle one)

Kindness Challenge

Donate an item to someone in need.

Date __/__/__

One moment that I really enjoyed today was...

Draw something that makes you happy:

1. _____
2. _____
3. _____

name 3 things you are thankful for today.

TODAY I FEEL

(circle one)

── *Inspirational Quote* ──

"A bad attitude is like a flat tire. You can't go anywhere until you change it

Date __/__/__

One moment that I really enjoyed today was...
_____
_____
_____
_____
_____
_____

Draw something that makes you happy:

1. _____
2. _____
3. _____

Name 3 things you are thankful for today.

TODAY I FEEL
(circle one)

―― *Inspirational Quote* ――

"You don't need a cape to be a hero. You just need to *care*."

5 Minute Girls Gratitude Journal

Date __/__/__

One moment that I really enjoyed today was...

Draw something that makes you happy:

1. _____
2. _____
3. _____

Name 3 things you are thankful for today.

TODAY I FEEL
(circle one)

— Memory-Making Challenge —
Have a paper airplane contest.

5 Minute Girls Gratitude Journal

Date
_ _|_ _|_ _

One moment that I really enjoyed today was...
_____
_____
_____
_____
_____
_____

Draw something that makes you happy:

1. _____
2. _____
3. _____

Name 3 things you are thankful for today.

TODAY I FEEL
(circle one)

Inspirational Quote

"Girls who read will one day lead."

5 Minute Girls Gratitude Journal

5 Minute Girls Gratitude Journal

Date __/__/__

One moment that I really enjoyed today was...

Draw something that makes you happy:

1. _____
2. _____
3. _____

Name 3 things you are thankful for today.

TODAY I FEEL
(circle one)

Memory-Making Challenge
Poke holes in a shoe box and collect different bugs on a walk.

5 Minute Girls Gratitude Journal

Date _ _ / _ _ / _ _

One moment that I really enjoyed today was...
___
___
___
___
___

Draw something that makes you happy:

1. ___
2. ___
3. ___

Name 3 things you are thankful for today.

TODAY I FEEL

(circle one)

― *Memory-Making Challenge* ―

Complete a crossword puzzle.

5 Minute Girls Gratitude Journal

One moment that I really enjoyed today was...

Date __|__|__

Draw something that makes you happy:

1. _____
2. _____
3. _____

name 3 things you are thankful for today.

TODAY I FEEL
(circle one)

Kindness Challenge
Do an extra chore.

5 Minute Girls Gratitude Journal

Date _ _ | _ _ | _ _

One moment that I really enjoyed today was...

Draw something that makes you happy:

Name 3 things you are thankful for today.
1. _____
2. _____
3. _____

TODAY I FEEL
(circle one)

—— Inspirational Quote ——
"Every day is a blank page to write your life story."

Date _ _ / _ _ / _ _

One moment that I really enjoyed today was...
_____
_____
_____
_____
_____

Draw something that makes you happy:

1. _____
2. _____
3. _____

Name 3 things you are thankful for today.

TODAY I FEEL

(circle one)

Memory-Making Challenge

Try to jump rope 100 times.

5 Minute Girls Gratitude Journal

Date __/__/__

One moment that I really enjoyed today was...
_____
_____
_____
_____
_____
_____

Draw something that makes you happy:

1. _____
2. _____
3. _____

Name 3 things you are thankful for today.

TODAY I FEEL
(circle one)

Memory-Making Challenge

Do a cool science experiment that you found on the internet (get your parent's permission for this one because it could get crazy or messy)

5 Minute Girls Gratitude Journal

We hope you enjoyed
your gratitude adventure

Discover more titles from Creative Ideas Publishing

CPSIA information can be obtained
at www.ICGtesting.com
Printed in the USA
BVHW020829130423
662290BV00004B/164